THE ROUTE NINE ANTHOLOGY

A Collection of Writing from Wesleyan Students, Faculty, Staff, & Middlesex County Residents

Compiled & Edited by Oliver Egger

Route 9 Literary Collective &
Wesleyan University Press
Middletown, Connecticut

Wesleyan University Press
Middletown CT 06459
www.wesleyan.edu/wespress

Route 9 Literary Collective
Middletown CT 06457
route9.org

Cover Design by Io Ilex
Logo Design by Leo Egger

Names: Egger, Oliver, editor.
Title: The Route Nine Anthology / Oliver Egger
Description: Middletown, Connecticut : Route 9 Literary Collective & Wesleyan University Press, 2022. |
Series: Wesleyan Poetry | Summary:
"A collection of poetry and prose from across Wesleyan University and Middlesex County, Connecticut"—
Provided by publisher.
Identifiers: ISBN 978-0-8195-0060-1 (trade paperback) |
ISBN 978-0-8195-0061-8 (e-book)

5 4 3 2 1

CONTENTS

Dear Reader,

Thank you so much for grabbing a copy of *The Route 9 Anthology.* This collection of poetry and a little prose represents a small glimpse into the literary talent of Wesleyan University and its surrounding community. This collection includes work from a range of voices, including: award-winning professors, dedicated students of literature, poet-laureates from various cities across Middlesex county, and local residents who write in their free time. Despite these differences, all these write interact in some way with this small county in Connecticut, which the 40.89-mile Route 9 connects from beginning to end.

In my first semester at Wesleyan University, Tony Connor, an Emeritus English Professor and contributor to this book, told me how, during his time at Wesleyan, he would organize theater productions that included faculty, staff, students, and local residents. I loved the idea of people from different backgrounds and levels of formal education all on a single stage engaging with and creating meaningful art and was inspired to create a similar space of literature. While it would take a pandemic, a few years, and a lot of learning about the Wesleyan and the local literary scenes, I am thrilled that a new single stage of art and community is here in the form of this book.

I am so grateful to you, dear reader, for engaging with this collection. I hope you witness the words and beauty that makes up our little university and little stretch of land we call home here in Central Connecticut.

With Love,

Oliver Egger
Anthology Editor
Wesleyan University Class of 2023

Local Color

Susan Allison
Long-time Middlesex County Resident,
First Poet Laureate of Middletown, CT

The neighborhood is full tonight.
We walk, hang out,
talk to strangers about
why they call that building the Arriwani
or watch that same strange man dance
when they play music in the garden.
"How in tune he is," you say, "how beautifully
he dances." Some of the tourists call him drunk,
but not you—
you see things differently.
You see old bottles lying around
in the gold, dried grass
like hobos, full of emptiness
and shining in the sun.
Sometimes you climb mountains
deep in thought
and you don't even notice
until you see valleys stretch out before you
and it takes your breath away—
the valleys are deep and green,
like an enormous ocean
frozen into steep crested waves
and you are suspended above it,
instantly timeless.
You recall the last time it happened—
when you met Marylin on Main Street,
who talks in thirty-foot long-jumps.

You found yourself stranded between her thoughts,
staring at the great valley
while she went ahead, hopscotch down Main Street—
woman who makes the hills and the mountains
by leaping with the moon,
muttering nonsense with her lips.
And when she shows up late for the music
the two of you greet like the sidewalk
legends you are, lost luminaries
who've survived imagination's demise.

§

Susan Allison (6/12/1961-5/15/2018) was Middletown's first Poet Laureate and co-founder of The Buttonwood Tree/North End Arts Rising, Inc.

Inheritance

Sahara Sidi
Wesleyan Class of 2022

I wasn't much older than you when the maggots hatched
from somewhere deep in our mother. They swarmed in

her throat. Made a faucet of her mouth and doused us
in gasoline. She said it ran in the family like a wildfire.

Which is really her way of warning us we could die
from the flames or let the smoke steal our last breath.

Our great-grandmother wanted to run but she stayed
in the garage until the smog of exhaust fumes took her away.

And believe me, I wasn't much older than you when I saw
our parents as people. Not as tooth fairies but the pliers

wedged in raw gums. Ready to harvest whatever is left
of another god damn bleeding mouth. Understand that

something like the devil has beckoned us to pay back
all that debt sewn into charred flesh and lord knows

not even a drunk man's blood could outrun this
kind of haunting. I come to know my unborn

in the mourning lights of a Planned Parenthood and
how fitting: my first declaration of love is a bloodletting.

§

Sahara Sidi is a Rackham Merit Fellow pursuing an MFA in poetry at the University of Michigan. Her writing has been recognized and supported by *The Adroit Journal,* The National YoungArts Foundation, and Wesleyan University's English Department.

Mercy, Mercy Me

John Murillo
Wesleyan Faculty
Director of Creative Writing

Crips, Bloods, and butterflies.
   A sunflower somehow planted
in the alley. Its broken neck.
   Maybe memory is all the home
you get. And rage, where you
   first learn how fragile the axis
upon which everything tilts.
   But to say you've come to terms
with a city that's never loved you
   might be overstating things a bit.
All you know is there was once
   a walk-up where now sits a lot,
vacant, and rats in deep grass
   hide themselves from the day.
That one apartment fire
   set back in '76—one the streets
called arson to collect a claim—
   could not do, ultimately, what
the city itself did, left to its own dank
   devices, some sixteen years later.
Rebellions, said some. Riots,
   said the rest. In any case, flames;
and the home you knew, ash.
   It's not an actual memory, but
you remember it still: a rust-
   bottomed Datsun handed down,
then stolen. Stripped, recovered,

and built back from bolts.
Driving away in May. 1992.
What's left of that life quivers
in the rearview—the world on fire,
and half your head with it.

§

John Murillo is an Assistant Professor of English and Director of Creative Writing at Wesleyan University, where he teaches the best poetry students in the country. He's also written some decent books. Google him.

First Date

John Kilian
Middlesex County Resident

She changed my life when she agreed to go
to Harbor Park after the show.
I do not remember what we ate,
maybe nothing, it was late.

Down the boardwalk for a stroll
Our hearts together spared us from the cold.
A late April weeknight, the park was empty,
but for us two meeting discreetly.

At the school where we worked
the children learned fast
of our love growing
and built to last.

The girl I held in Middletown's harbor
anchors me to Middletown forever.
When our children ask where to find true romance
I will tell them the river is your best chance.

§

John Killian has lived in Middletown twenty five years
Time enough to sail its waters
And drink its coffee.

Mark Rothko: Ochre and Red on Red

Ben Togut
Wesleyan Class of 2023

In front of the mirror
another self Golden

body Screen of morning
light You'd never know him

Boy as old as the century
slipping into new clothes

The sun warmed
him scalded him

like the best lover   How I envied him
He gave his body away like summer

The flowers exhale
their fragrance I inhale

memory I was touched
I was silk the light

bled through

§

Ben Togut is a poet and singer-songwriter from New York City. His recent work is published or forthcoming in Flypaper Lit, The Offing, Hobart, and elsewhere.

Novel Criminal

Alice Ghislaine Musabe
Wesleyan Class of 2022

The night before my appointment
felt like the shortest nap of my life.
The twenty-minute drive was apprehensive,
no words uttered between my mom and me.
But our hearts surfaced with terror and dissonance,
my decision became a village decision
and I was called a criminal and killer.

I found solace at river shores.
Hoping that mother nature is looking after my baby,
bonding with hundreds of girls and their babies there.
Societal discourse amazes me; it's cynical
In the 1800s, pregnant girls were drowned,
now I am the bad guy– the killer.

At night, I hear a grasping cry.
My friends bombarded me with "what ifs…?"
I have lost interest in sex since then,
and I run away from the frigid village,
I take a walk by the river shore.

I want to bear my Blessing,
and raise my Happiness,
However, I'll never know who I carried
or what struggles I would have carried into the world.
But now it will always be named my Brave
until I can bear my Blessing.

§

Alice Ghislaine Musabe is a poet and aspiring clinical psychologist. She grew up captivated by mental health and later on found a way to combine her mental health interests and professional aspirations into poetry. Most of her poems revolve around themes of mental health, feminism, and love. She uses poetry to heal herself and her audience.

Three Poems

Douglas Martin
Wesleyan Faculty
Assistant Director of Creative Writing

January

meaning to search for: repost
fingers go "repot"
rethink then what thought

*

your note came after
night snowfall
forming us

how many inches of this
white looking for something
green to smell.

forget all the ghosts
trusting to sleep beside you
winter howling wind

*

coldest night of the year
can hear the dog's heart thump
your worried sleep sounds

plant grow light clicks on
behind laptop playing
FUTURE TIMELAPSE

February

if only up an hour
earlier I would have seen
less cars on the work walk

*

walk round the park
to see what kind of
procrastinator to be

plastic flower where
the dog pees
now that the snow has melted

*

cold night curl
in borrowed bed
into fetal position

*

the old couple walks together.
I trail behind
their public need

March

post-midnight walk to borrowed bed
snow quiet before
loud work nightmares

*

from my feet to your
face cat moves as we
come to different wake levels

*

like planted, uninflated
balloons the tulip
blooms: white, yellow, purp.

§

Douglas A. Martin is the author of some ten books of poetry and prose, most recently *WOLF,* an anti true crime novel.

A Writer's Welcome

E. Lenore Milling
Former, Long-time Middlesex County Resident

Naked, skinny trees
shivering in the wild,
whipping wind,
branches creaking in the quiet night,
owls perched frozen,
eyes open and unkind,
as stars give off
a cold winter's light:
this is the season when all
the flowers die,
and the songbirds fly,
to where the sun
still shines,
couples walk the city streets,
huddled and hurried,
searching for heat,
starving have-nots
line up for something warm to eat,
where the pigeons and
ministers and bums
all meet,
small children wrapped like
gifts in wooly hats and long
scarves, wait for
the school bus, staring into
passing cars,
young hippies
and old punks

spark fires in the park,
whilst the moms
stay mollified
in their apple-
scented homes,
and the dads rush off
to try and make their mark,
and the old folks
sit together
in the dim-lit coffee shop
lamenting their
younger selves
as they wait
for their hearts
to stop,
and the bitter chill of
the wind stays true,
while squirrels
frantically scramble,
still having much to do,
and the clouds race by
against a sky
of the dullest blue.

§

Ebony Lenore Milling is a poet, painter, and florist. A long-time resident of Middletown, she now lives in Eugene, Oregon. She writes under several pen names including E. Lenore Milling and Ebony M.

My Uncle Died on Mammoth Mountain

Jane Hollander
Wesleyan Class of 2023

At least there is the solace
that he was dead before he hit the snow, but imagine
watching a man dropping fast
against the blue sky
against the narrow evergreens of the Sierra Nevadas,
feeling that final thud shake
your conscience, shake
that huge volcanic mountain
and send a ripple over the lakes.

§

Jane Hollander is an English major and Environmental Studies minor. She enjoys running, hiking, farming, reading, and long conversations with friends.

American Jihad

Zubaida Bello
Wesleyan Class of 2022

There is no passing here—
Of time, of bodies
my youth eats at this landscape
redraws casualty as a swollen lump
a desert spoilage.

I dream of lost things
My ghost limbs: gunpowder/ artillery/ dusted/ this land?
A new foreign
/This corpse?
An old resting place

Tomorrow, Uncle Sam punctures
My skin.
We call this inspection
Tomorrow, I will stretch my hands
beyond this battle.
We call this "flight".

Today, signs search for me,
build me
from a crow's wing;
Oscillating
A stolen rubble.

Yesterday, we dream of pretty things:
Flat surfaces,
Rolling pastures

Camouflage, a reappearing act.
Everything, fertile.
Tombstones can't grow here.

§

Zubaida Bello is a member of the 2019 NYC Slam Team, a Mellon Mays Fellow, and a James Baldwin Scholar. She has performed original poetry at The Apollo, The Met, New York Live Arts, and The United Nations. Zubaida has published articles in *The African-American Point of View, YB Heard, Asterism*, and *Chalkbeat.* Zubaida uses her poetry as an outlet for trauma, a form of activism, and to reimagine the world that she has inherited. *How to Stop the Burning,* her debut chapbook, focuses on femininity, family, intergenerational trauma, and blackness.

If I make you go against yourself

Ren Ellis Neyra
Wesleyan Faculty
Associate Professor of English

You cry wolf, when you're the (mf) wolf, heifer—
democracy-now-ass, repair-as-transcendental-signified. Go get ass!
But no night I've known rolling at the club unmade the third space of the law what it is:
lawless. And you (I mean, who calls porn absolution for imperialism? Force fluff?)
will remain you. So, worry not your episteme. Fetishize this: if
war is written into peace, and the world is charged with the grandeur of its
flame-out, then you'll remain intact, narrator of "doom"TM. I.e. en lieu of l'avenir's
history, let there be ruse. Let there be, pangs schooled at forepangs. Grief
discarded ad infinitum. Oh, but do keep your ringer on! May thy selfhood never chafe.
(What would make those ish-ists say afterlife—
fathom it; you can't with your fair-weather head—
Irreparable injury's dramaturgs—the real, fantasmagoric—O, thou Terrible—
When all they mean to say, or, sedimented in the false subtlety is a yearning for slavery.)
How you're not found out when you keep toying around with the proverb ("dead-
ass"), fuck around and find out...

§

Ren Ellis Neyra is an Associate Professor of English at Wesleyan University. Most of the time, Ren writes essays, and sometimes poems.

Poem for Juneteenth Celebration, 2021

Naji Chester-Payne:
Middlesex County Resident
Poet-Laureate of Portland, CT

WHAT IS IT I DID
I'VE BEEN A CONTRIBUTING CITIZEN
SINCE I WAS A KID
KEPT OUT OF JAIL
NEVER CAUSE VIOLENCE
MOVED LIKE A MOUSE
AND STAYED REALLY SILENT
I HAVE HOPES AND DREAMS THAT I'VE TRIED TO REACH
LISTENED TO THE WORDS OF ALL I'VE HEARD PREACH
FROM THE PROFESSORS THAT TEACH IN THE SCHOOLS AND THE STREETS
READ THE WORDS OF THE BIBLE AND ALL OF THE CONSPIRACY THEORY LEAKS
THERE'S SO MANY MORE PROBLEMS THEN THE SKIN I AM IN
TIMES I HAVE TO MOVE LIKE IM WALKING ON PINS
REAL SLIGHT LIKE A NINJA, BUT I STILL FEEL THE PAIN
ON TOP OF HATES,
EVOLUTIONARY HEART STAIN
I DIDN'T LIVE AS A SLAVE, NOR THE 40S TO 60S
I WATCHED VIDEOS THAT HURT MY SOUL
FOREVER
THEY HAVE CHANGED ME
HISTORIES PAST HAS TAUGHT US TO SURVIVE
PERSISTENCE HAS TAUGHT US HOW TO THRIVE
A UNFAIR CLIMATE BUT ADAPTABILITY IS WHAT GOD PROVIDES
LESSON LEARNED FROM ANIMALS,
TOGETHER WE ARE STRONG
A SIMPLE EQUATION WE ALWAYS GET WRONG
WE HURT OURSELVES WHICH MAKES US WEAK
A BATTLE WE ALL LOSE OVER "BEEF"

FOLD IN YOUR THUMB
CRINKLE YOUR FINGERS OVER YOUR PALM
RAISE YOUR FIST HIGH
WISH THE PAIN TO BE GONE
FROM THE SOUL, WITH TEARS IN YOUR EYES
FEEL THE HORRIBLE PAST OF YOUR ANCESTORS TO THE SKY
LET IT GO, FREE AND LET BE
INJUSTICES BRUTALITIES THROUGHOUT ALL HISTORY
THE MISERY IN THE TRUTH
THE SUFFERING IN ALL LIES
IS PEACE REALLY REAL OR IS THE WORD GOING TO DIE.....
TODAY, TOGETHER , LET'S TRY
NOW OPEN YOUR HAND
AND FEEL LOVE
LET'S ALL KEEP PEACE ALIVE
FEEL THE LOVE, LET'S ALL KEEP PEACE ALIVE

§

Naji is the Poet Laureate of Portland, CT, a personal trainer, an organizer of community events, a fork truck driver, and a handsome single dad. He gets inspired from everything in life and the beyond. To him its always about all the questions: who what where when why and how.

how to stop losing at poker

Casey Epstein-Gross
Wesleyan Class of 2025

lose

and then lose again.
lose your keys.
refuse all help.
lose your keys
and do not call
a lockpick. lose
your home. you
are homeless now.
lose your wife
because she does
not like that you
are homeless now.
lose your job
because they do
not like that you
are homeless now
either. lose your
jacket and enlist the
drunk who crashed
his car into the lake
to find it. listen
as he tells you that
he calls himself
Tequila Sunset. lose
your name. call
yourself Winner
instead. lose

your body heat
in mid-november,
lose the grass of
your makeshift bed
by mid-december.
squat in a room
with half a wall
missing. get arrested
for loitering. lose
your freedom. lose
it all barring the bars
of your cell and the
chips in your hand,
the cards up your
sleeve that no one
sees but you. no
one sees but you.
lose. lose. lose. lose
and lose again,
you're good at it now,
so keep losing, keep
losing, lose and lose
and lose—until the
memory of poker is lost
too. until all that remains
is the smoke
clogging your arteries,
the bumps on your
tongue that feel like
sand, and the faintest
inkling of some vague
glassy memory that
seems to suggest that

loss
once tasted like blood.

§

Casey Epstein-Gross is a student at Wesleyan University, where she was recently awarded the Sophie and Anne Prize for Poetry and is the Assistant Poetry Editor for *The Lavender,* Wesleyan's literary magazine. Her poems have appeared or are forthcoming in *Sugar House Review, Permafrost, Thin Air, Soundings East,* and other journals. She can often be found eating Baked Lays, wearing olive green, being self-referential, and rambling about Veep's Amy Brookheimer.

Route 27, morning

Sophie Griffin
Wesleyan Class of 2023

They came upon a crest in the highway, a raising that gave the three a new vantage point. Up ahead, a perfect circle, a disc cut out of the sky, pale red contrasting with the surrounding yellow. It was 5:15, or maybe 5:30, and the sun was just coming up. She, the driver, pointed up at it, remarked it looked like they were on Tatooine. Something about it seemed too correct, a shape stolen out of Plato's world of Forms, surreptitiously stashed under a coat and smuggled out and hung up in the sky by someone who reached up on their tiptoes, pushed a single thumbtack through to keep it in place. It got redder through the morning.

She kept driving, following the light early morning traffic through the scrubland along the side of the one-lane highway. Everything was tinged a bit pink, and she couldn't help but think of the strangeness of it all, the otherworldly nature. Maybe they'd driven through a wormhole back at that intersection with the long reds, into another planet with another sun. Maybe that sun wasn't mostly hydrogen, but burned off neon, changed colors throughout the year. Maybe kids on that planet remembered Christmas as purple, March as bright orange, the long summer months as green sliding into blue. Maybe.

She accelerated a little, willing the white car forward, a little closer to the one in front of it. Soon they'd three be in the ocean. Would the breaking lines of waves reflect the sky? Would there be perfect circles floating on the surface of the water for seabirds to cut through as they dove for breakfast, for curious minnows to swim up to, for surfers to lean off their boards and drag a searching hand through? Or would the light refract, scatter out, before their toes made it to the sand and the water and they floated out, no longer supporting their own weight?

§

Sophie Griffin is a junior at Wesleyan University from Long Island, New York. She likes to wake up early.

clawfoot

Sallie Hayden Bianco
Middlesex County Resident

Okay then, You notice, when stepping out of bed, that your foot hurts in a peculiar manner. This can happen for any number of reasons. Say you stepped on a sharp stick, for example. Or maybe you jammed it into an empty soup can. Maybe you were in a plain ole 'fit of rage' and caught sight of the can accidentally. Then you thought, "Oh, Perfect!" Naturally, no shoe comforts such a foot after a stunt like that. The podiatrist takes a look. You notice his severely thick eyebrows rising up high. Far too high. "I don't know how to tell you this. But it appears that your foot is turning into a claw." Well well well…

§

Sallie Hayden Bianco grew up in Tempe, Arizona, and later attended Smith College in Massachusetts. In 1976 she met Tony Connor in her Middletown, Connecticut Mexican restaurant, La Boca. Quickly he began helping her with plays for Wesleyan University and other bits of nonsense.

from *A Library of Light*

Danielle Vogel
Wesleyan Faculty
Associate Professor of English in Creative Writing

,

We come to life now. When we. When we are. We pick up language like a lit garment, wet and shaken out. A shinbone lifts. An elbow. A paragraph. All shot through until our edges dissolve in pleats. We are held together through our separatenesses. We are an ambiance of remains. Wreckage, re-configuring. We are an illuminated architecture. Nothing you know to name. We are a moving letter. Topologies of sound. We are never static, but echoic. As we make shape, we take it. The mouth, unmarooned. We trespass punctuation. A curvature. An arc, unarchived in the sharing. We almost make a circle, but what we mean is silence into sound. Or a coming into focus. We are always in the present tense. The flood of the gap, washed out. We, a word. We, a window. Bring your body.

,

When we are six, we are also seventeen. When we are six, we are reading. But we cannot yet read. Our language drapes over some thing and we make shape associatively. When we are seventeen, we are reading by resonance. A certain rhyme in the curve of an atom. The slight of it slips through the tongue. A leaning of throats. When we are three, we are also fourteen. When we are fourteen, we do not know the difference between a book and a body. We are unbound, gutterless. A woman's skin near the eye. We are a page, the plum-colored aureole. A cobbled finger-bone, a vague star system.

,

A slope of cells. Or water, stories. A soft warping through the gloss. A belly. We refuse to come into convergence. We are already converged. We are the yellow hour that laminates the horizon. We are a strigosing of selves. We love. When we are. When we are there. When we are one, we are sometimes also twelve. When we are three, the ground is mostly ether. We walk through the specter of things. When we are seven, the world is drained. When we are only four, we live in empty hours. When we are six, we fall in love with the position of a sun, the slats between astronomical bodies. We fall in love. We love through the throat. We reverberate. We are wedded in occurrence. We are led by our hands, but we have no hands. When we are nine, we are also twenty. We are a shifting geometry, the rotation of a sound, and the halo moves from the window.

,

,

When we are. When we are there, we lay together and cover ourselves with our voices. When we are ten, we are also twenty-one. We speak of breathing, but this is a thing we cannot do. When we are seven, we are also eighteen. When we are eighteen, we begin our bodies. But we are unmappable, unhinged. A resynchronization of codes, the crystalline frequencies of stars, seeds, vowels, lying dormant within you. We are the oldest dialect. A sound the voice cannot make but makes.

,

,

When we are not yet born, we are also ten. We feel our birth a thousand miles away. We see a body suspended across the sky. We come cleaved at birth. We are both zero and eleven. We are an irregularity draped across a country. We are here, we say. We are here. We are uncusped at the threshold. Tangential at the curve. A compendium of skins. A skinning sound. We are flooded. We are emanated. We are a mesh of strings, striated, invisible. We are a single canopy. A permeable membrane, molecular, wet at the lips.

,

,

We want you to reach for us. We are the alphabet realigned, unarchived against the body. We say, this is a book. A body. We say, this is a sentence. We say, my mouth is a living record. We say, a bright lattice-work, a netting. We say, watch. We watch this net breathe as it reconfigures itself between us. We say, this is a thing that makes shape and takes it. We say, this is not a border, or bed. We say, inlets. Sound.

§

Danielle Vogel is the author of *The Way a Line Hallucinates Its Own Linearity, Edges & Fray,* and *Between Grammars.* She is an Associate Professor at Wesleyan University, where she teaches workshops in innovative poetics, memory and memoir, the lyric essay, and composing across the arts. She also runs a private practice as an herbalist through which she offers consultations and botanical remedies. Vogel makes her home in Connecticut on the ancestral lands of the Hammonassets and Wappinger peoples, with her partner, the writer and artist, Renee Gladman.

By Happenstance: A Tale

Patricia H. O'Brien
Middlesex County Resident
Poet-Laureate of Old Saybrook, CT

Her name is Princess, his, Jose. Her hair, painted
wild berry, traverses her face with every breeze. When I offer
to take the selfie they're trying to take, we chat a bit, as is anybody's way.
When I warn that their faces will be lost in the shadow of the water's glare,
Jose says he doesn't care ... they need to pose there before the sea,

their likely disappearance the price they'll pay. Every year now, Jose says,
they journey to Westerly, despite how sad he gets as they pass the house
of his friend's mother, now deceased. He'd helped his friend take care of her.
He loved her and is sad every time. Yes, every time. But glad, too, he says ...

They rode their motorcycle here, I learn, as I
contemplate *Reverse* in my Subaru and cocktails ahead.
The rough blare of their engine heats up the lot's black top.
Roughs up everyone's sign-off ears.
    Their music, blasting confident,
                rouses the evening's drowsy heat.   Lifts gulls' wings.

All late winter, early spring, I stormed the beach, breath
steaming curses against the cold, pretending myself warm. Damning
the useless sun. Today the sun brought Jose and Princess,
my erstwhile useless curses undone. And as the sun bows out

to eventide, Jose and Princess, helmets strapped and certain
for the Interstate, roar away in opposition to the lot's arrowed path,
repainted last season ... faint but, nonetheless, able to convey
the safe way.

His friend's mother's house, empty still, awaits
their passing by. He'll nod then, even as they fly away,
Princess's escaping hair
                                        banner of love's constancy.

§

Pat is a graduate of Columbia School of Social Work. She's a member of the Guilford Poets Guild and co-founder of CT River Poets. She has helped in the establishment of Prison Hospice in three CT prisons where they facilitate poetry workshops. She initiated the ongoing program, Paintings and Poetry, at Florence Griswold Museum. Her first collection of poetry, *When Less Than Perfect is Enough,* was published in 2012. She and her son, Richard Manders, co-wrote and published their memoir about their adoption journey, *The Laughing Rabbit: A Mother, a Son, and the Ties that Bind* in 2018.

The Pigeon

Oliver Egger
Wesleyan Class of 2023

A pigeon struts on the gray
concrete of the hospital window
ledge. My brother, only thirteen,
twitches, jerks up, pulls at
the white wires which swirl
from his small head. Eyes
opened, unseeing, swollen
from a midnight mind. Wrists
bound by a thin white
rope to the corners of the
bed, all blue and black
from yanking at the sand
of his skull. He stares out.
He screams, 'Come back.'
'I'm not going anywhere'
–I start but it's not for me,
it's for the shadow
of the pigeon who had
launched away to the
paradise of anywhere else.

I watched a home video
taken right before
birth. It was all the same.
The shoes are by the door,
the old dog is curled
by the radiator, the ghost
of my father's coat, heavy

on the hook. And my brother,
a toddler, is hooked around
my mother's legs. She is
heavy with me and pats our
body as if wondering what waits
in these unwritten words, this
innocent child. God. I see
my brother, the whole mass
of madness before him, he
pokes my mother's belly.
He stares. He laughs. He speaks
to me with a pigeon gray voice,
'Don't you wanna live? Don't you
wanna live?'

§

Oliver Egger is the editor of this thing and a fan of poetry since his father made him memorize ten poems to get his first mountain bike. He is the founder and editor-in-chief of the Wesleyan student literary magazine *The Lavender* and his work can be found in *Moonstone Press, Oyster River Pages, The California Quarterly,* and more. Maybe one day he will give up poetry and pursue a mountain biking career.

Song of Solomon

Amy Bloom
Wesleyan Faculty
Director of Shapiro Writing Center

Kate stood in front of the mirror trying on dresses. She could almost get into her black suit, but that couldn't be right for the New Year and it was almost eighty outside. She put on a yellow sleeveless dress with a white linen blazer and white sandals. Too summery but not bizarre. Do they wear hats? In church, women wear hats. Do Jewish women wear hats? Kate stared into the mirror, sweating in her slip, milk starting to come through her nursing pads.

Not now, she thought. If I nurse the baby, I'll be late for the ceremony —no, the services. Be calm, you must nurse the baby, Dr. Sheldon would want you to nurse the baby, you can tell him that you were almost late because you had to nurse Sarah and he'll smile. Kate relaxed, thinking of his smile, like a cool cloth on her cheek.

Okay, we're all right. Kate took off her yellow dress, laid it out, and called to Sarah, who was just starting to make her little sucking noises, "It's okay, Mommy's coming, everything's okay." On her way to the baby's room, she grabbed a towel and looked on the top shelf of the closet for her white cartwheel straw hat. God did love her. He knew she had to get to the temple. The hat was there, and it was unblemished and unbent.

Kate looked at Sarah and felt the milk slide under her bra, down her rib cage. "Here we are, little duck. Mommy's baby. Dr. Sheldon's perfect girl." She picked Sarah up and changed her, watching herself move smoothly and competently, like a Pampers commercial. Sarah didn't wiggle, just knotted her toes in Kate's long blond hair. She plunked down in the rocking chair with Sarah and nursed her, wincing for a second as that ruthless, sweet mouth clamped down on her nipple. She watched Sarah and she watched the clock.

"Okay, Sarah beans, ten on one, ten on the other, and then we're out of here. Going to temple. Going out today, Miss Sarah." While Sarah took a short break between breasts, Kate grabbed a clean blue dress from the laundry basket and put Sarah into it.

We're almost there, Kate thought. Come on, plan ahead. Plan it so you don't screw up. Okay, she finishes nursing, I burp her, on the towel. I put her in her crib while I get dressed, my shoes are not in my closet, they're still in the hall closet. Okay, we're walking down the hall—no, the diaper bag. The diaper bag is in Sarah's room and it's already packed, with another dress. Good girl, Kate. Okay, we have a fed baby, a diaper bag, a dressed mother. The hat, the hat is still in the closet, you don't put it on until you get there and you can see what they wear.

Make-up. You put your make-up in your purse, your whire purse sitting on the hall bench, ready to roll. All you need is a little lip gloss and some cover-up for your raccoon eyes. You're all right. He doesn't care for make-up. Remember, in the hospital, sitting on your bed, he said that he didn't care for make-up and that you didn't need it anyway.

Kate closed her eyes, to remember better what he said, his saying it, to feel the weight of his body at the end of the bed, her bare feet almost touching his hip.

The whole seventy-two hours in the hospital Kate's body was never dry. She was damp and awake for every sunrise, her wet nightgown twisted up around her waist. Blood, milk, and sweat streamed over and through her. The night nurse had told her to get up and walk, but she was terrified that when she stood up her organs would just fall out, the cut muscles and tissue crumbling away like rotted newspaper.

"I promise you, you start walking now, when all the other ladies are home taking Percoset you'll be pushing Miss Sarah around the block. I'll take that catheter out now, too."

She saw the nurse's smooth, thick hands flick back the heavy hem of her nightgown, and she shut her eyes when she felt the slight emptying tug.

"All right, let's roll."

Let's roll, Kate thought, and stood up, wanting her voice to match the nurse's light bounce. Let's roll on out of here. She could hear the crowds cheering in her head as she walked down the hall, the i.v. rack skittering alongside her, the nurse's hand gently pulling on her good arm. She felt the shimmery heat of his presence before she really saw him, his back to her, talking to the nurses at the coffee station. They were barricaded behind twin coffeepots, personalized mugs, wide open doughnut boxes.

Kate shook off her nurse and strolled, with great effort, toward the coffee station.

"Wonderful. You're walking already, isn't that wonderful?" Dr. Sheldon turned to the nurses, who smiled politely; they didn't care if she walked or not, and Kate didn't care about them either. If she didn't say something, he'd be gone, and she was too tired to stand around waiting for the right moment.

"Could I speak to you?" The sweat slid from her under-arms right down to her feet, wetting the paper slippers they'd given her.

"Of course. I'll save your nurse a trip, even if your quality of care suffers a little."

The nurses all smiled; he was a corny old guy, but nice. He practically lived in the maternity ward. His patient, the new mother, looked like she was about to pass out, and Kate's nurse went to grab a cup of coffee before the inevitable call.

He put his hand around her bicep, and Kate could feel the blood rushing from her arm to her cheeks.

"The nurses like you," she said, looking at the passing room numbers so he couldn't see her face.

"Yes? I like them. It's hard work, they're terribly understaffed. First there weren't enough nurses because they were paid so badly. Now there aren't enough nurses because it costs the hospitals too much to keep a full shift."

Kate smiled. Even though her back ached and she could picture each of her twenty stitches clearly, lighting a hot, narrow torch across her belly, she beamed. He gripped her arm a little tighter, and as her face went white and the walls around Dr. Sheldon began to spin, she smiled again and he smiled back before he called the nurse.

Sarah had stopped sucking a little sooner than usual, and Kate was so grateful she sang to her all the way through burping. Everything went smoothly; little Sarah, stoned from nursing, was completely content to lie in her crib and murmur to the world. Kate dressed like a surgeon prepping, precise and careful in every movement. She checked her watch again. Twenty-five minutes to get to the temple. She had driven there yesterday and timed it; it was only fifteen minutes away. Five minutes to find a parking space, five minutes to get Sarah out of her NASA-designed carseat and into her Snugli. Forget the Snugli, in a summer dress and a blazer you can't carry a baby in a blue corduroy Snugli. Okay, no Snugli. I carry her in my arms, wrapped in a yellow and blue blanket, to show off her eyes and her hair. Fine.

Kate moved through all of her steps, locked the front door, and got into the car, strapping Sarah in with the blanket tucked around her, supporting her soft boneless neck.

"We're rolling now. Off we go, into the wild blue yonder, flying high into the sky ... " Sarah had fallen into one of her instant naps, from which she would emerge charming and alert but not yet hungry. Perfect for seeing Dr. Sheldon.

Kate didn't even look pregnant until her sixth month. The other women in the library began to talk to her a little, to tell her things. They had left her alone all summer, feeling that whether her silence was due to a bad attitude, problems at home, or painful shyness, she was too much trouble. Pregnant and single and willing to take anyone's advice, Kate was not too much trouble. "Go to Dr. Sheldon," they said over lunch in the back room. "'He's the best." Especially for the weird, the dispossessed, the single mothers, the ones who wished they were, the ones who needed to talk at two in the morning, not just about their babies. And when Kate met Dr. Sheldon and he didn't purse his lips when she said she had only met the father once and hoped she never would again, she knew that she and the baby were in the right place. When he helped her out of her chair, she felt ethereally beautiful and as delicate as baby's breath, her ankles and heartburn forgotten.

She drove up to the synagogue and was appalled to see millions of cars. It looked like an airport terminal, women and children piling out of backseats, all the women wearing hats. Kate laid her hand happily on the white hat next to her, perfect for her blond hair. He'd like it. She could tell he liked her hair from the way he commented on Sarah's duck fuzz. "Not much now," he said the night he sat so close to her, "but she'll have your curls by the time she's one." The men were pulling away from the entrance, craning their necks to find parking spaces. They weren't wearing hats, of course, just those little beanies—what were they called? She could ask Dr. Sheldon. Unless he'd be offended by her ignorance, rather than charmed by her interest? Please let him find me charming, and my daughter irresistible.

She was damp and rumpled by the time she found a spot behind the A&P. She scooped up Sarah like she was going for a touchdown and trotted toward the temple, hugely domed and out of scale between a sandwich shop and a dry cleaners. A block away, Kate slowed down, licked her lips, and smoothed the front of her dress with her free hand. Please.

He was standing on the sidewalk talking to some other men, but alone. No wife. She would put one of those St. Jude ads in the paper, the kind that said, "Thank you for helping me. Now I need you more than ever." She shifted Sarah to her left shoulder, lined up her purse and the diaper bag on her right shoulder, and smiled the way her mother had alway wanted her to.

"Why, Dr. Sheldon."

"Ms. Tillinghast. What a surprise, what a pleasure. I didn't know we belonged to the same shul."

Kate thought quickly, circling the strange word. "I've never been here before, actually, but I've wanted to come for a long time. I hope nobody will mind the baby, my regular sitter couldn't make it." Kate smiled self-deprecatingly, showing that she knew some people didn't like babies and would consider her careless for having brought Sarah. But Dr. Sheldon wouldn't think so, which was why she had told Joan not to come today.

"No, of course not. Who could object to this angel, this proof of God's goodness?"

As he bent his head toward Sarah to kiss the back of her round moist head, Kate felt so happy she thought her heart would break through her chest and fly around the temple, like a dove released.

They squinted at each other in the September light, smiling and wondering what the other person saw. Dr. Sheldon thought Kate saw a pallid, overweight man sweating in an old navy blue suit, black-rimmed glasses sliding halfway down his big nose and wild gray curls floating around his bald spot. She didn't; she saw God. Kate thought he saw a slightly crazy woman, wild with exhaustion and loneliness, but he didn't see that. He saw that her dark blue eyes lit up when they rested on his face and that her hand lay tenderly, unconsciously, on his sleeve, like a lily. He saw that their house would have white flowers and bright plastic toys on the floor. He would not be alone.

"People are starting to go in," he said.

"Oh." She sounded wounded, which alarmed him. Had he offended her? Maybe she didn't want to sit with him.

Dr. Sheldon shuffled backward, to show that he hadn't meant to intrude, and Kate's eyes filled with tears. How could he be leaving now, now that they were together?

Sarah thrust one pink foot through her blanket, and they both looked at it, flexing in the air. Kate's face was so filled with loss and love that Dr. Sheldon reached out for her, and she pressed his hand to her hip as they carried Sarah up the temple stairs.

§

Amy Bloom is the Shapiro-Silverberg Professor of Creative Writing and Director of the Shapiro Writing Center at Wesleyan University. She is the author of three New York Times best-sellers and three collections of short stories, a children's book, and a ground-breaking collection of essays. She's been a nominee for both the National Book Award and the National Book Critics Circle Award.

Ode to Your Kia

Sabrina Tian
Wesleyan Class of 2024

I used to ride shotgun with
my knees touching the glove compartment.
And whenever we stopped in some parking lot
made private by the dark,
I would open it up, take out
your hands, turn them around,
gingerly now,
feel those rough calluses
on my fat lower lip, try
to grow my palm as wide as yours
to match and fail.
I remember thinking I'd write a poem about the wrinkles on
your knuckles and how they might hold
the wisdom of ten ancient trees.
    They said I would write great poems about you.
We'd loved in your car more than once.
I think the sheer size of your animal body
and the quake of my deepest breaths ever
stretched the whole thing out.
    I wouldn't have minded putting
    my arm through the window or
    my head through the roof, but it's
                    your car, not mine. You know,
                    you told me how somebody robbed
                    your car right before we met and
                    I can't believe the only things they left behind
                    were some salmon sushi
                    and those damn hands in the glove compartment.
After our first time, I had no appetite for days. I think

my stomach was full of all those great poems
and at that point, I couldn't bring myself to ask,
"Will you pull it out of my throat?"
In some effort to purge myself, I read you what poems I already had and you said,
"Wow, seems like he did a number on you."
How do I tell you that I only write poems about people who "do numbers" on me?!
I felt lighter in the moments after, but in the end
I shut the door with a heavy belly.
So sincerely, I thank you
for helping me make some extra space.
I needed the leg room on the ride back home.

§

Sabrina Tian is a sophomore at Wesleyan University majoring in East
Asian Studies and Government. She loves Wes Anderson movies,
Richard Siken poems, and Rauschenberg combines.

For Beginners

William Ollayos
Wesleyan Staff
Wesleyan Residential Life Area Coordinator

To guide the missing...

Blood to blood,
and heavens crossed,
shield thy eyes
with Jude the lost.
Into, under,
and between,
the saint can find
in the unseen.
Moonlight and silver,
women nor men,
blood to blood,
we call again!

To correct injustice...

Golden rays upon
the sweet angel,
under the Sun
that shines so bright –
find salvation
in the darkness,
encased in the
liquid grip of Night.
So God bless this wandering child,
so dear Goddess make it right.

To enliven the dying...

Feathers and
Glitter irritate
The spaces
Between my
Fingertips
While pterodactyls
Scream in my
Skull.
Chandelier lights
Wept this
Tinsel onto my
Cheeks.
Everyone is a
Bird of prey and
I
Want to go
Home.

To expose...

Great Earth Shaker,
I call you near
To raise all treasures
Buried here.
Dip briny hands to the ocean floor
And let these secrets hide no more.

§

William Ollayos works for the Office of Residential Life at Wesleyan University. Find him in North College or at Freeman Athletic Center throughout the week. Ask to see pictures of his dogs!

Across The Street

Tony Connor
Middlesex County Resident
Wesleyan University Emeritus Professor

Mr. Hubbard and Arthur argued,
father and son at each other's throats,
disputing results of football matches,
routes of canals, names of streets,
who played when, on which instrument,
in Cheetham Hill Prize Brass Band,
the name of the King's youngest brother,
the exact depth of Clowes Park pond.

Any old thing could set them off;
I sat by their kitchen fire in awe
of claim and counter-claim and insult
friendly-furious, getting nowhere –
nowhere near fracture, broken bond.

I watched, I listened: a close-lipped lad
who lived across the street, right opposite,
in a silent house without a dad.

§

Tony Connor was born in 1930, in Manchester, England. He left school at fourteen and was apprenticed to the textile trade, in which he worked for sixteen years as a designer. From 1948 to 1950 he served in the Fifth Royal Inniskilling Dragoon Guards, with the British army of occupation in Germany. Later he taught in an art school, a technical college, and a bakery, while making many appearances on TV. He has published twelve books of poems and was elected a Fellow of the Royal Society of Literature in 1974. From 1971 to 1998 he was a professor of English at Wesleyan.

Summer 2019

Sofia Baluyut
Wesleyan Class of 2023

A cool breeze riff and the double-time drums
roll across the roof like credits, and we have graduated,
I am wearing that purple sweater, and framed
by skyscrapers, a friend climbs higher than he should

and we reach towards him, laughter bubbling
from our bellies, from something stronger
than the beer, hands up like praise, he takes
a picture. This summer will teach me

the sound a pigeon's bones make
under the crush of a car, the shriek
it pulls raw from my throat

the smell of my hands, their hospital
tremble, my grandfather's hair
still strung on the teeth of a comb, and how

grief catches like thin clothing
on some sharp and waiting doorframe,
draws blood on every page I write, but here,

there is the boy atop the watertower,
and, I promise, I'm not retelling this wrong,

he does not jump. He does not fall.

§

Sofia Baluyut is a poet from Brooklyn, NY.

Waterbody

Emily Hollander
Wesleyan Class of 2023

Across the river, a little iceberg
lapped, inch by inch--no--particle by particle,
translated back to the language of the vessel,
just as we form our flesh, every seven years, shedding
forever regenerating the present,
and so, suddenly,
the gulls on their icy floating homes
have never seemed so lonely, I am sure
the wind blows them to opposite ends of the earth, and
I cannot say why this scares me
perhaps because I have never let go of your hand,
or, only once have I opened my mouth,
let the wind enter, and pictured my many twins,
her, and the stars and the water, and these seagulls
who seem so lonely, but perhaps just know more than I do
about letting the current hurl you home,
about severing flesh from bone

§

Emily Hollander is a poet majoring in English and Environmental Studies in addition to competing on varsity Cross Country and Track & Field. When she is not running or writing, she enjoys painting, hiking, and farming at Long Lane.

Notes

All the pieces in this collection are previously unpublished except for:

"Local Color" by Susan Allison, which was originally featured in *Down by the Riverside Ways* (Antrim House, 2009). Rights reserved to and permission granted by Stephan Allison.

"Mercy, Mercy Me" by John Murillo which was originally published in Poem-a-Day on May 1, 2018, by the Academy of American Poets. The piece was later featured in *Kontemporary Amerikan Poetry* (Four Way Books, 2020). Rights reserved and permision granted by Four Way Books.

"Song of Solomon" by Amy Bloom, which was originally published in *Come to Me* (HarperCollins, 1993). Rights reserved and permission granted by HarperCollins.

Acknowledgments

Thank you, first and foremost, to all the amazing writers whose work makes up this anthology. Your work inspires and moves. Thank you to Stephan Allison who submitted work on behalf of his late wife and first poet-laureate of Middletown, Susan Allison. And thank you to Io Ilex for her stunning cover.

Thank you to Anne-Marie Cannata McEwen of the ButtonWood Tree in Middletown for her support on this project. Thank you to Rhea Drozdenko and the Wesleyan Jewett Center for Community Partnerships for their support from the Innovation Fund. Thank you to the Middletown Arts Council and, in particular, Kisha M. Michael and Lee Godburn for their support. Thank you to Jeremy Cutler for his emotional and logistical support.

Thank you deeply to Suzanna Tamminen, Editor at Wesleyan University Press, for giving me the opportunity to make this book a reality. Thank you, Jaclyn Wilson and Stephanie Elliott Prieto at Wesleyan University Press for their support and kindness, as well.

Thank you to my teachers of literature at Wesleyan: John Murillo, Susanne Fusso, Marguerite Nguyen, Amy Bloom, Natasha Korda, and Edwin Sanchez. Thank you to my teachers of literature back home in Durham: Barry Blanchett, Ms. Nile, Mr. Cross, Ms. Garvoille, Ms. Wimberly, and Ms. Barbaza. You have all inspired me so much.

Thank you to The Route 9 Literary Collective and everyone in the community of literature that we have made together at Wesleyan. In particular, thank you Emily Hollander, Jane Hollander, Immi Shearmur, Cate Levy, Bell Rush, Victoria Dozer, and Annie Wendorff for being my rocks. Thank you also to Jack Stewart and Jake Neuff, who helped me back in early 2020 to brainstorm this project.

Thank you to my friends who supported me throughout this project. Thank you Ani Bryce and the whole Bryce family, Zack Hersh, Kate Ciolkowski-Winters, Tobias Matz, Anabele Demartino, Lana Kalfas, Sarah Albert, Mary Ahlstrom, Lila Blaustein, Ruby Baden-Lasar, Maggie McCormick, Rory Curtin, Abigail Seevak, and many more.

Thank you to Myraim Arvelo; you made me who I am.

Thank you to my family. To my parents, Helen and Daniel, for all their love and teaching me a love for life and literature. To my siblings Sasha and Rebecca for their brilliance and inspiration. And to, most of all, my twin brother Leo, my rock and my best friend.

And lastly, thank you, dear reader, for your time and your wonder.

CPSIA information can be obtained
at www.ICGtesting.com
Printed in the USA
BVHW030506220822
645067BV00002B/5

9 780819 500601